In Search of Saint Alban

by

Simon Webb

First published by The Langley Press, 2010

ISBN  978-0-9564551-4-7

The cover shows a medieval pilgrim badge of St Alban, reproduced by
kind permission of Steve Millingham:  www.pewterreplicas.com.

Pictures marked 'WM' are from Wikimedia Commons

# CONTENTS

Greater love hath no man than this,
that a man lay down his life for his friends.

John 15:13 (KJV)

# I: A ROYAL VISIT

Some time around the year 793 AD, the city of St Albans received a royal visit from a king called Offa.

Offa was an Anglo-Saxon king, and the Anglo-Saxon period in England often saw the country divided up into many small kingdoms ruled by petty kings. Offa could not, however, have been characterised as a petty king. By means that are still unclear, Offa managed to expand and consolidate his kingdom so that at one point he seems to have gained control of much of the south of England. He even demoted other kings from the status of monarchs and turned them into men of lesser rank, subordinate to himself.

As well as dominating southern England, Offa was able to play a part on the European stage – letters exchanged by Offa and the emperor Charlemagne are some of the earliest records of English diplomacy. The reformed coinage that Offa introduced was based in part on Charlemagne's coins.

One surviving sign of Offa's power is Offa's Dyke, an immense earthwork built by the king to separate his own kingdom of Mercia from the Welsh kingdom of Powys. Despite the passage of over twelve hundred years, the Dyke is still eight feet tall in some places, the earth wall looming over a deep ditch.

The Anglo-Saxon kings were descendants of Germanic invaders who, about sixteen hundred years ago, began to take over large areas of what we now call England. England and the English were named after one Anglo-Saxon group, the Angles. Many of these first English people were warriors at heart, and they used gifts, particularly curiously-worked artefacts in precious metals, to secure the loyalty of their warlike followers. It may be that Offa came to St Albans with a chest of glittering trinkets to give out to the locals, but he is also supposed to have *found* a much stranger and more important treasure, right there at his destination. He found the remains of the local saint, who had been martyred outside the Roman city of Verulamium half a millennium before Offa's time.

It may seem an odd thing to do, to disturb the sleep of a long-dead saint, but the bones of saints and martyrs were often 'translated'. St Cuthbert, the seventh-century monk and bishop, was first buried on the holy island of Lindisfarne off the coast of Northumbria, but the monks of that place later took his bones with them as they fled the Vikings. Cuthbert sojourned at Chester-le-Street for many years before finding his final resting-place under the flagstones of Durham's Norman Cathedral. St Bede, now Cuthbert's neighbour at Durham, was translated from Jarrow by a pious eleventh-century thief called Elfrid, who pursued the hobby of collecting and translating holy bones, often without the consent of their original guardians.

Whether or not Offa really found the bones of Alban, he was such a formidable ruler that few people would have been foolhardy enough to question his discovery at the time. In any case, the witnesses to the spectacle of Offa's followers digging up St Alban would probably have been too busy trying to take in the religious and political symbolism of the king's grand gesture.

According to the legend, the king was told in a dream where to find the saint's bones. The more learned inhabitants of the area would immediately have drawn comparisons between Offa and the many characters in Biblical and later Christian stories who were favoured with divinely-inspired dreams. These include Joseph, who was told in a dream that he should marry Mary, the mother of Jesus (Matthew 1:20). St Peter was also told that he could abandon the Jewish dietary laws, in a strange dream where he saw a profusion of animals of different types held up in a cloth (Acts 10:11-13). Another important dreamer in the Christian story is Constantine, the Roman emperor who, shortly before he became emperor, was granted a dream or vision of a Christian symbol, which inspired him to make life easier for Christians when he became ruler of the Roman world.

By discovering a holy relic, the location of which had supposedly not been known before, Offa might also have put the more educated residents of St Albans in mind of St Helena, mother to the aforementioned Emperor Constantine. When her son was emperor, Helena travelled to the Holy Land and discovered the cross Jesus had been crucified on, under a Pagan temple which had been built on the site of Golgotha.

It may seem far-fetched to speculate about eighth-century English people thinking of Helena, a saint born in what we now call Turkey, but as far as the English were concerned, Helena and her family were part of British history. According to a version of her story related by the twelfth-century historian Geoffrey of Monmouth, Helena was the daughter of King Coel of Colchester – the 'Old King Cole' of the nursery rhyme. Constantine's father Constantius is supposed to have married Helena, on which occasion, if it ever really happened in Britain, King Cole would no doubt have called for his pipes, and his drum, and his fiddlers three.

By making the family of Constantine an essentially British family, albeit with a continental immigrant as the father, the old chroniclers were expanding imaginatively on the fact that Constantius did spend time in Britain, and even died at York, in 306 AD.

The Anglo-Saxons were very much aware that the country they had seized from the Britons had once been a Roman province. They lived their lives among Roman ruins, and often travelled on the arrow-straight Roman roads. There is an Anglo-Saxon poem called *The ruin* which laments the passing of the grand times enjoyed by the Romans in an unnamed city with a celebrated bath-house – probably the city we now know as Bath in Somerset.

As well as increasing his own personal prestige by 'discovering' the body of Alban, Offa was simultaneously boosting the fame of the place where he had found it. In Roman times, Verulamium was one of the more prosperous British cities, situated near the Roman road now called

Watling Street; a city important enough to have been burned to the ground by Boudicca in 61 AD. Offa may have seen in this historic place somewhere to rival the great cities of Europe, including Canterbury, the cradle of English Christianity.

It seems that the Anglo-Saxon king from Mercia had a certain amount of influence in Kent, but that he resented the fact that Canterbury was such an important religious centre within England. The importance of Canterbury was due to the fact that it was there, at the end of the sixth century, that St Augustine had set up a sort of bridgehead from which he sent further missionaries to many parts of England. Offa's resentment of the status of Canterbury inspired him to push for the large, historic diocese of Canterbury to be split up, and, as a result of his influence, the new diocese of Lichfield was established. Lichfield was traditionally regarded as the site of the mass martyrdom of over a thousand Christians in the third century: indeed, some think that 'Lichfield' means 'field of corpses', and that the name refers to this massacre. By drawing attention to Lichfield, and also to St Albans, Offa was perhaps trying to trump Canterbury as the most ancient seat of Christianity within the Anglo-Saxon kingdoms. Yes, he might have said, Canterbury was where *English* Christianity started, but there were saints and martyrs in these islands long before we English ever came here.

King Offa founded or re-founded an abbey at St Albans, and by doing so he put himself into the already long tradition of pious English kings who had founded or enriched monasteries and churches. Those early missionaries under Augustine had adopted the wise strategy of converting the local kings first, in the expectation that, once they had become Christian, they would encourage their subjects to become Christian also. A good example of this type of Christian king was Oswald of Northumbria, who died in 641. Oswald imported monks from Iona to preach to his people and, because they didn't speak the local language, the king even translated the Word himself, standing up next to the preaching monk. Later, Oswald died in battle against the Pagan prince Penda. He was made a saint, and his head is thought to rest in the tomb of St Cuthbert at Durham.

Throughout the Middle Ages, it was important for any major Christian centre to possess the relics of at least one saint, and it can be said of many great cathedrals throughout Europe that they might not exist if the bones of some saint or martyr were not thought to lie within them. The presence of the sleeping saint often provided a name for the religious foundation, and reminded local worshippers that someone who rested among them had achieved a great measure of religious perfection. Local magnates making donations of land, money or further holy relics to the church would often donate them to the saint by name, and the holy bones could become a focus for long-distance pilgrimages. Pilgrims were the ancestors of modern-day tourists, and by various means the local church and the local people could make money out of these visitors.

By bringing St Alban to light, and causing an abbey to be founded or re-founded over his body, Offa was, to use a modern metaphor, 'priming the pump' for centuries of devotion and pilgrimage. But what exactly did he do with Alban's bones when he made his royal visit?

Matthew Paris, a thirteenth-century monk of St Albans, has left us a picture of Offa directing two depressed-looking peasants as they dig the shrouded form of St Alban out of a patch of wild grass. Modern scholars have questioned the assumptions behind Paris's picture, and have sought to minimise Offa's role in discovering Alban's bones.

In his *Ecclesiastical history*, the Venerable Bede tells us that, a few years after Alban's martyrdom, when the Emperor Constantine made Christianity legal throughout the empire, a beautiful shrine was built over the remains of Alban. This shrine was still in existence when Bede was writing, only sixty years or so before Offa's visit. This seems to be inconsistent with the idea of Offa 'discovering' Alban, and has thrown doubt on the Offa story: how could anyone discover something when its location was already known to everyone? In Runcie's *Cathedral city: St Albans ancient and modern*, Martin Biddle suggests that Offa did little more than translate Alban from a grave in the earth into a tomb above ground. Biddle's version takes the miraculous element out of the Offa story, but leaves us with the power of Offa's grand gesture.

The eighteenth-century martyrologist Alban Butler insisted that the

9

Pagan Anglo-Saxons destroyed the original church that covered Alban's bones, but if this church was still in existence in Bede's time, then it seems a little late in history for Pagans to be roaming around wrecking Christian buildings.

## II: FLESH ON THE BONES

By drawing attention to St Alban as he did, Offa was shining a bright light on a page of British history which, frankly, has very little written on it that can still be read. The evidence to support the story of St Alban is pretty slender, and the earliest writings on the first martyr of the British provide only the barest bones of a story.

The first mention of Alban in the historical record appears in the *Life of St Germanus*, a hagiography or saintly biography written by one Constantius of Lyon around the year 480, a date perhaps 180 years after Alban died. This Constantius should not of course be confused with Constantius Chlorus (meaning 'Constantius the Pale') who was the father of the Roman emperor Constantine the Great.

Germanus, the subject of Constantius' biography, had been a lawyer and a soldier, but the people of Auxerre (then called Autissiodurum) begged him to become their bishop. This he did, and in the course of transforming himself into a religious leader, he cast off his wife and embraced the ascetic lifestyle, deliberately punishing his body in order to benefit the progress of his soul. To this end, he slept on ashes and wooden planks, and even ate ashes as a starter to his frugal meals of self-baked barley bread.

Germanus became an important part of British history in 429 AD, when he was sent to Britain by Pope St Celestine I to combat the Pelagian heresy, which was then gaining ground among the British. The Pelagians were followers of Pelagius, a revolutionary preacher, perhaps born in Britain, who probably died in Palestine just a few years before Germanus was sent to the land of the British. Pelagius promoted a version of Christianity that was more self-reliant than that then being promulgated by the Roman Catholic church. In particular, he recommended an ascetic lifestyle, which may be why the hard-living Bishop of Auxerre was thought to be the ideal man to combat Pelagianism. The physical presence of the hair-shirt-wearing Germanus might have reminded the Pelagians that not all Roman Catholic prelates lived the kind of pampered life that Pelagius had scorned.

By performing many miracles, and winning a formal debate with the Pelagians that may have been held at St Albans itself, Germanus believed he had suppressed Pelagianism in Britain. As it turned out, he had to return to these islands in 447 to defeat Pelagianism again. At the formal debate in 429 the Pelagians are supposed to have turned up 'flaunting their wealth, in dazzling robes, surrounded by a crowd of flatterers'. If this is true, it seems that they had forgotten the ideas about the simple life promoted by Pelagius himself. They must have made quite a contrast with Germanus, who wore the same cloak and tunic all the time, regardless of the season, and usually wore them until he had completely worn them out.

In his *History of Roman Britain*, Peter Salway tells us that excavations at St Albans have revealed a large open space, in use in the fifth century, which could have been the venue for the debate Germanus won so decisively. As if to cap off his victory against the Pelagians, Germanus miraculously restored the sight of a blind child right in front of them.

It seems that Germanus visited Britain just at the time when the British (meaning the Celts of Britain) were beginning to have serious problems with the Anglo-Saxons who, according to the old legends, had first been invited in as mercenaries to help the British fight against their northern neighbours, the Picts. According to one story, Germanus led the Britons into battle against a combined army of Picts and Saxons, teaching them the battle-cry 'Alleluia!', the sound of which caused the enemy to run away. At that time, the Britons were Christian, whereas the Anglo-Saxons still clung to their Pagan gods, such as Tiw, Woden, Thunor and Frige. The names of these particular gods have survived in the modern English names for Tuesday, Wednesday, Thursday and Friday.

According to some texts of Constantius's biography of Germanus,

Alban appeared to Germanus in a dream, and told him the story of his life. Modern editors of Constantius's text, such as Wilhelm Levison, and F.R. Hoare (who translated the hagiography into English) believed that the saints' lives, such as those of Alban and St Genevieve, that appear in Constantius were inserted by other hands as many as four hundred years after Constantius wrote his book. In his pared-down edition of Germanus' *Life*, Hoare therefore includes some passing references to St Alban, but no complete life-story of the saint.

If Hoare and Levison are right, then the original version of Constantius's book contained the first mention of St Alban to survive in the historical record, but not the first re-telling of his story. In any case, the early versions we possess were probably all based on an even earlier account of the life of Alban, called the *Passio Albani*, which now only survives in later copies.

As a miracle-worker, Germanus seems to have specialised in identifying and banishing devils who had possessed people, and making people float in the air as if suspended on ropes. The ninth-century historian Nennius writes a lot about Germanus in his *Historia Brittonum*, but, strange to say, he doesn't mention St Alban. In Nennius, Germanus shows his supernatural talents by correctly predicting the immediate death of a man, and also the destruction of a city by a thunder-bolt. When himself and his companions are served a complete roast calf for their dinner, Germanus tells his fellow-diners not to eat any of it. The next morning, the calf is alive again and standing outside with its mother.

Gildas, a sixth-century British writer, includes a version of the life of Alban in his book *De excidio Britanniae*, a Latin title which is usually translated as *On the ruin of Britain.* By the time Gildas was writing, the Anglo-Saxons who had been scared off by Germanus's war-cry had taken over much of the Britons' land, and forced the British themselves into what we now call Wales.

Gildas's book is not so much a history as a lament (or even a rant) about how the laziness and general wickedness of the British had given the Anglo-Saxons the opportunity to gain so much ground. In the same way that Geoffrey of Monmouth turned Helena into a British-born saint, the writers Gildas drew on turned the Roman emperor Tiberius into a very unlikely champion of Christianity. It was supposedly by his influence that Christianity was spread to Britain, but his good work was undone by the 'tyrant' emperor Diocletian, who persecuted the Christians.

Gildas tells us that, like the British martyrs Aaron and Julius (of whom practically nothing is known) Alban died during the persecution of Diocletian, which was so widespread and brutal that it is still called the Great Persecution.

In Gildas's version, Alban sheltered a fleeing Christian 'confessor' in his house, put on the man's cloak to disguise himself as his pious house-guest, and, as a result, was taken out to be executed. Before the sword touched his neck, Gildas's Alban performed a miracle when the river Thames parted to led him pass. The man detailed to decapitate Alban converted from a Pagan lion to a Christian lamb on the spot, and was also executed.

During the miracle of the parting of the Thames, Gildas's Alban walked between walls of water like precipices. This might strike most readers as an obvious parallel to Moses' parting of the Red Sea, but Gildas recalls instead another Biblical parting, of the River Jordan, which is recounted in the Old Testament Book of Joshua (Joshua 3:17). On this occasion, the priests carrying the Ark of the Covenant dipped their feet in the water of the Jordan, only to find it risen up into a heap upriver, so that they and all the Israelites could cross on dry ground. Gildas may have thought of this miracle instead of that of Moses (Exodus 14-16) because the Thames and the Jordan are rivers, unlike the Red Sea. Gildas had of course made a mistake about the name of Alban's river – St Albans lies in the valley of the River Ver, not the Thames.

Alban's parting of the River Ver would have had an extra significance for any Pagan Romans or Romano-British people who witnessed it. Valuable objects found in the Ver suggest that the locals regarded it as a god, and sacrificed trinkets to it in Pagan times. If nothing else, the Christian God's ability to tame the river may have demonstrated that the

14

new God of the sky had power over the old gods of rivers, lakes, streams, forests and mountains.

Writing nearly two hundred years after Gildas, the Northumbrian scholar-monk Bede added several crucial details to Alban's story. In his *Ecclesiastical history*, completed in 731, Bede tells us that when Alban sheltered the Christian cleric, he himself was a heathen (meaning a Pagan). Bede also gives Alban time to be brought round to the Christian way: Bede's text implies that the cleric remained hidden in Alban's house for several days at the very least.

Bede introduces us to a character not mentioned specifically by Gildas – the unnamed 'judge' who questions Alban about his identity and orders him to sacrifice to Pagan idols. Alban disappoints this man and is soundly beaten by his agents.

On his way to be executed, Bede's Alban is watched by a huge crowd of people of both sexes who are inspired by God to witness the martyrdom. Bede places the river (unnamed in this version) between the town walls and the 'arena' where the execution takes place. The executioner who converts on the spot is moved to do so partly because he witnesses the miracle of the river.

During a pause in which a new executioner decides to take up the sword, Alban climbs a beautiful flowery hill overlooking the arena. There a spring miraculously appears, and flows just long enough for Alban to quench his thirst. When the new executioner strikes off the saint's head, his own eyes drop out. The miracles surrounding Alban's martyrdom persuade Alban's judge to abandon the persecution of the Christians, as well they might. Bede, like Gildas, also mentions the obscure martyrs Aaron and Julius, and gives us the names used by the Anglo-Saxons of his day for the old city of Verulamium – Uerlamacæstir or Uæclingacæstir.

Although Bede doesn't specifically mention any baptism for Alban, he may be implying that Alban was baptised when he mentions that the executioner-turned-fellow-martyr was baptised in his own blood.

In writing his account of Alban, Bede may have had access to some version of the original *Passio Albani*, and he certainly used both Gildas, and Constantius's *Life of St Germanus*. The Northumbrian, who was much more like a modern historian than Gildas, may also have sent off to St Albans for more information – we know that he did some of his research by correspondence, and he even had colleagues rummaging through archives as far away as Rome itself.

Bede's reputation as a historian, as well as the level of detail in his account of St Alban, make these pages of his *Ecclesiastical history* something approaching the definitive account of the first British martyr. After Bede, everyone either followed Bede or elaborated the story in ways that owe more to fancy and error than to research.

The details added by the twelfth-century chronicler Geoffrey of Monmouth include names for the immediate persecutor of Alban, whom he calls Maximianus Herculius, and for the priest who hides in Alban's house, whom he calls Amphibalus.

The priest's name seems to have been derived from Geoffrey's confusion over the Greek word for the type of cloak worn by the priest – a cloak with a sewn-on hood known to the Romans as a *caracalla*. The Roman Emperor known by the nick-name 'Caracalla', who will appear again in our story, was so called either because he had designed this type of cloak, or because he habitually wore one.

Maximianus Herculius, better known as Maximian, was a Roman emperor who ruled jointly with Diocletian, after Diocletian had introduced a system whereby the empire was ruled by four men: two Augusti and two Caesars. Maximian was one of the Augusti, and he took the extra name Herculius when he was promoted to that position. Geoffrey of Monmouth, or the authors he used, may have assumed that because Maximian ruled during the time of the Diocletian persecutions, and because he was known to have visited Britain, he must have been the judge who condemned Alban to death.

The ultra-Protestant John Foxe, in his best-selling sixteenth-century *Book of martyrs,* does well to stick closely to Bede's version, but he separates out the miraculous parts of the narrative 'because they seem more legend-like than truth-like' and leaves them 'to the free judgment of the reader, to think of them as cause shall move him'. Foxe complains about a fanciful version of the martyrdom of Alban supposedly produced by a Pagan contemporary of the saint, which Foxe asserts was probably written by a monk of St Albans. In this version, when the river dries up, the people who had drowned in it over the years are found at the bottom, still alive. Angels are also seen ascending and descending in a pillar of fire, and Alban's head speaks after it has been cut off.

John Foxe also mentions the obscure martyrs Aaron and Julius, but he claims they were martyred at St Albans and not, as earlier writers implied, at Leicester, Carlisle, or Caerleon in Wales. Although he warns that this part of his story may not be reliable, Foxe also reports the fate of Amphibalus, the priest Alban sheltered. Foxe says that this saint escaped into Wales, but was then captured and brought back to St Albans, where he suffered a prolonged and agonizing death. Although these details of the last days of Amphibalus are likely to have no basis in fact, the adventures of 'St Cloak' do reflect something Bede writes about – attempts by British Christians to escape the emperor's persecution by hiding in hills, mountains, forests and caves. This would have been much easier in Roman Britain than it would be today, as the whole of Great Britain was then home to only a few million people, and there were still many primeval wildernesses, including vast wetlands only navigable in small, shallow boats.

Butler's *Lives of the saints* gives a very full account of Alban, which is not surprising when we consider that the eighteenth-century Catholic priest who wrote this massive work had 'Alban' as his own Christian name. Drawing on the writings of sixteenth and seventeenth century scholars, Butler gives us a picture of Alban before his martyrdom as one of the leading citizens of Verulamium, able to afford to travel to Rome as a young man, for the sake of his education. Butler gives a name for the executioner who refuses to behead Alban – Heraclius or Araclius – which he derives from the writings of the fifteenth century scholar-monk, John Capgrave. Father Alban also gives us more details about St Amphibalus's escape into Wales – apparently he took a thousand Christian converts with him, but these were all 'cut to pieces by the idolators for their faith'. In this version, Amphibalus himself is stoned to death.

In a footnote, Butler refers to the cloak of St Alban, kept in a chest at Ely, which was opened during the reign of Edward II. At that time, the blood at the top of the cloak was still fresh, as if it had just been spilt.

Following the chronicler John Stow, who died in 1605, Butler gives us more detail about King Offa that modern historians would be likely to trust. He says that Offa ruled over more than twenty counties, including half of Hertfordshire; that he made a journey of devotion to Rome, and that he insisted that his subjects pay 'Peter's Pence', a tax payable to the pope. According to Stow via Butler, Offa did not collect this tax from his beloved abbey at St Albans, an abbey that was founded during a great council at Celchyth, attended by, among others, 'fifteen bishops, with several kings, governors and noblemen'.

It is hardly surprising that later writers should have tried to put flesh on the bones of Alban's story. As it stands in Bede's version, we know practically nothing about the saint apart from the circumstances surrounding his martyrdom, and the fact that he had a house. We would like to know if he was a native Briton who had adopted a Latin name, or if he was an immigrant from some other part of the empire. Was he, as Geoffrey of Monmouth's Constantine was supposed to be, a man of mixed Roman and British blood? What was his occupation and status? Was he married? If he started the story as a Pagan, did he worship the old British gods or the new Roman ones, or both? How old was he when he died? All these questions can only be answered by reference to the imagination.

The Emperor Claudius (WM)

Septimius Severus (WM)

Eusebius (WM)

Diocletian (WM)

Diocletian's palace at Nicomedia (WM)

The execution of Alban
(Miranda Brown, based on a picture by Matthew Paris)

Offa finds Alban
(Miranda Brown, based on a picture by Matthew Paris)

John Foxe (WM)

St Helena (WM)

Constantius Chlorus (WM)

Constantine at York (Gunnar Larson/WM)

Bede (Miranda Brown, based on a manuscript illumination)

Walls of Verulamium (Kurpfalzbilder/WM)

## III: VERULAMIUM

Modern scholarship and archaeology can add little to the story of Alban's martyrdom, except to fill in some of the background details of the picture, particularly those that have to do with early Christianity in Britain, and with Roman Verulamium itself.

In old Roman cities like London, the modern city was built on the ruins of the ancient one, which makes archaeology very tricky. By contrast, the edge of modern St Albans stands close to the site of Roman Verulamium, but the two places are quite separate. Since the Saxon and Medieval cities of St Albans grew up around the abbey Offa founded or re-founded, it seems that at some point the site of Verulamium was all but deserted, and the people moved east to be near the shrine of their saint. This is similar to the movement of the population in Medieval Rome, where the people clustered near the Vatican in the north-west, and large areas within the city walls became farm-land.

At the height of its importance and prosperity, Verulamium seems to have been an impressive example of a Roman city. In his article on Verulamium in Runcie's *Cathedral city*, Sheppard Frere presents his argument that the Roman city continued to operate as a city well into the fifth century. Since it was already a Roman city in 61 AD, when Boudicca burned it down, it was already nearly two and a half centuries old when Alban met his end.

Frere puts the date of the founding of the Roman city at 49 or 50 AD, but he explains that the site of Verulamium was an important settlement even before the Romans came. It was a major centre for the Catuvellauni, a tribe of Britons who later moved their capital to Colchester. Some coins issued by a ruler of the Catuvellauni called

Tasciovanus also bear the name Verlamio, which may be what the Catuvellauni called what we call St Albans. When the Roman Emperor Claudius invaded Britain in 43 AD, both Colchester and Verlamio were conquered by his forces, and it seems that the Catuvellauni may have made some sort of peace-treaty with the Romans.

The Roman city of Verulamium may have been founded as a reward for the Catuvellauni's peaceful submission to the new rulers of their world. In his *Annals*, Tacitus tells us that Verulamium was a type of city called a *municipium*. This would have been very different from a city of the *colonia* type, which is what Colchester became. At Colchester, Roman army veterans were in effect given a new city and much of the farmland around it. If Verulamium was a true *municipium*, then it would have been a Roman city inhabited by Romanised Catuvellauni, with an admixture of immigrants and sojourners from other British tribes, and from other parts of the Roman Empire.

The Romans rebuilt Verlamio and turned it into Verulamium, a city on the typical grid pattern that can still be seen in the old Roman city of Chichester. Although the place was burned down in 61 AD, and also partly burned down around 160 AD, Verulamium rose again from the ashes, perhaps even more prosperous than before. This tends to indicate that the city was a real city, able to support itself economically, and, unlike some ill-fated new towns throughout history, built in a suitable location.

The city had all the usual amenities of a Roman town, including public latrines continually flushed by flowing water. There were workshops turning out pottery, metal goods and jewellery, among other things. There were also bakeries and breweries. The city's walls were high and thick, and faced with hard flint, rising up over a steep, deep ditch. There were grand arches at several entrances to the city, which was split in two by Watling Street. There were shops strung out along the road and, in true Roman style, tombs and cemeteries along the roads outside the city walls.

There were public baths, and many fine private houses big enough to have their own suite of baths. Legal cases would have been heard in the

28

*basilica*, a Latin word for a type of large hall, that would only later come to mean a kind of Christian church. Taxes would also have been paid at Verulamium, in gold, which would have been bought in exchange for goods, or coins made of less valuable metals.

The fact that Verulamium was situated on a main road, only a short distance from London, surrounded by farm-land and containing workshops where various trades were practiced, would seem to indicate that Roman Verulamium was something like a prosperous modern English market-town.

If, as Butler claims, St Alban really was a prosperous citizen of Verulamium living there near the beginning of the fourth century, then he would have drunk water fed through wooden pipes, probably from an aqueduct. He might also have drunk the locally-brewed 'Celtic' beer, sometimes treating himself to a glass of imported wine. He may have eaten pork, and even hunted for wild boar. He would have shopped in the forum and watched performances at the theatre. He may have served as a city magistrate, in which case he would have been awarded Roman citizenship, which would have conferred on him certain privileges and protections under Roman law.

As a Roman citizen, or at least as a prominent citizen of the town, Alban may have met important official visitors, who would have been lodged at the city's *mansio* or government guest-house.

As for Alban's house, he may have lived in a spacious dwelling boasting many high-ceilinged rooms, with brightly-coloured frescoes on the walls, and mosaic floors. He may have had under-floor heating, in the form of a hypocaust system, to keep his feet warm in winter. In his house, he may have had pottery and cutlery either imported or made locally, and perhaps even glass vessels. He might have had bronze statuettes of the gods he had worshipped before his conversion to Christianity. No doubt these statuettes, and any Pagan gods depicted on the walls and floors, would have become increasingly embarrassing to Alban as his new faith took hold.

If he was living only in the city of Verulamium, and had no house elsewhere, Alban was probably not a member of the very highest stratum of local society. The really rich seem to have preferred to live in villas, surrounded by their own farm-land, at a reasonable distance from the city.

Some archaeologists have suggested that Verulamium reached its peak of prosperity and population long before the time of Alban and Diocletian, and that the many problems, including inflation, that affected the Roman Empire in the early fourth century might have caused serious decline in places like Roman St Albans. Other experts point to evidence of building and re-building within the city in the time of Diocletian, which would seem to indicate that the place continued to be prosperous and populous.

Although not all of the features discovered by archaeologists would have been thriving, or even present, when Alban was alive, the town did have several Pagan temples, including one probably dedicated to the worship of Rome itself, and of the Roman emperors, who were routinely turned into gods after their deaths. There is also evidence at Verulamium for a temple to the mother-goddess Cybele, and temples to Minerva, and her brother Mercury, patron god of markets.

While Pagan worshippers would have visited their temples openly, any Christians at Verulamium, in this time of persecution, would have met secretly, probably in the house of a member of the clandestine church. A meeting of these unfortunate believers may have been broken up by the soldiers, and one of those who escaped may have found himself pounding on the door of Alban, begging for refuge.

If Alban's pious house-guest was part of a local covert Christian community, then we must ask how there came to be Christians in Verulamium in the first place. There is, unfortunately, no reliable straightforward narrative for how Christianity reached Roman Britain. The old chroniclers, like Bede and Geoffrey of Monmouth, recounted the legend of an ancient British king called Lucius, who asked the second-century Pope Eleutherius to send missionaries to his kingdom. Unfortunately, the sources for this story were all written hundreds of years after it is meant to have happened, and modern scholars regard Lucius as a mythical king (although Eleutherius was certainly a real pope).

Another legend about the coming of Christianity to Britain involves Joseph of Arimathea, a man who is named in the New Testament. In the Gospels, Joseph is the one responsible for claiming Jesus' dead body from Pilate and taking it down from the cross with the help of Nicodemus, a powerful ally of the Jesus group. Joseph then conveyed the body, wrapped in fine linen and anointed with myrrh and aloes, into a new tomb he had cut out of the rock in his own garden (see Mark 15:45, John 19:39 and Luke 23:50-53).

The man from Arimathea gets a new lease of life in Medieval legend, beginning in the ninth century when Rabanus Maurus, the Archbishop of Mainz, tells us in his *Life of Mary Magdalene* that Joseph travelled to Britain as a missionary, accompanied as far as France by, among others, Lazarus and Mary Magdalene herself. Some stories even state that Joseph, as Jesus' uncle, may have visited Britain with his nephew Jesus, to buy tin from the Cornish mines.

Visitors to Glastonbury will have heard the story that the abbey there was founded by Joseph of Arimathea, and that a famous tree called the Glastonbury Thorn was Joseph's staff that sprouted and then rooted into British soil. Joseph is also supposed to have brought the Holy Grail to Britain, as well as vessels containing Jesus' blood and sweat. Joseph was helped in his mission to convert the ancient British by eleven other Christians – the whole group is supposed to have been sent by Philip the Apostle.

The story of King Lucius, and the much more elaborate stories surrounding Joseph of Arimathea, read like attempts to explain the fact of early British Christianity by introducing compelling characters and events into the narrative. The story of Joseph of Arimathea is an obvious attempt to link a New Testament character to the history of the faraway British Isles, islands which dwellers in the ancient Mediterranean civilisations thought of as the islands at the ends of the earth, if they thought about them at all.

Christianity is more likely to have come to Britain in the hearts of Christian immigrants from all over the empire. Our evidence for their lives lies in the existence of artefacts that have come to light over the centuries, many of which bear, or seem to bear, Christian symbols. An early example is a word-square found scratched on a fragment of pottery found in Manchester, in a location that seems to suggest that the fragment was placed there in the second century. The square reads:

```
R O T A S
O P E R A
T E N E T
A R E P O
S A T O R
```

This means 'The sower Arepo holds the wheels carefully', which is pretty meaningless, but the letters can be unscrambled to form the following cross-shaped arrangement:

```
                A

                P
                A
                T
                E
                R
A  P A T E R N O S T E R  O
                O
                S
                T
                E
                R

                O
```

This includes the Latin for 'Our Father', as well as Latin versions of the Greek letters Alpha and Omega (A and $\Omega$) – a reference to Christ (see

Revelation 1:8).

Cemeteries and buildings of a recognisably Christian type have also been excavated, and of course the stories of Alban and his obscure fellow-martyrs Aaron and Julius deepen the colours of our picture of Christian Roman Britain. Some have speculated that Aaron may have been a Christian from the Holy Land itself, descended from a Jewish family that had converted to the new religion. Certainly the name Aaron is not a Latin name, like the names Alban and Julius, or the names Celer, Paternus, Sacer, Sabena and Tacita: the last five names in this list were all found scratched on pieces of Roman pottery at Verulamium. Other Roman names found locally include Oastrius, and Lucius Arrius Caludus, potters who stamped their names on their wares, and Salonicus, who may have owned land and pottery-kilns between Verulamium and London.

## IV: SEVERUS OR DIOCLETIAN?

Gildas, Bede and Geoffrey of Monmouth all place the martyrdom of Alban during the persecution of the Christians by Diocletian near the beginning of the fourth century, but some doubts have been raised as to whether Alban actually perished then, or in one of the earlier imperial persecutions. Martin Biddle, author of the *Dictionary of National Biography* article on St Alban, argues that the saint must have died under Diocletian, because the city wall of St Albans is mentioned in the story, and that wasn't built until after the earlier persecutions. John Foxe also contributed to this debate when he stated, just after his treatment of the St Alban story, that the first nine persecutions of the church had not touched Britain, and that only the tenth, under Diocletian, had caused British Christians to lose their lives.

Frere insists that the martyrdom of Alban must have happened in 209 AD, during the reign of the emperor Septimius Severus, who was emperor from 193 to 211. Severus certainly ruled the empire at a time when persecutions happened in Egypt, Cappadocia, Antioch, Rome, Carthage, and possibly Corinth, but the persecutions of this emperor were neither as severe nor as widespread as those of Diocletian.

In 208, Severus came to Britain with his sons Geta, and the aforementioned Caracalla. While Severus and Caracalla were campaigning in Scotland, Geta, the younger son, was left in charge of the south. Frere argues that Geta 'evidently presided at the trial' of Alban, backing up his claim with the fact that Geta bore the title of Caesar: in some re-tellings of the martyrdom of Alban, his judge is referred to as 'Caesar'.

Severus became ill and died at York in 211, at which point Caracalla

34

became emperor. There was a deadly rivalry between the new emperor and his brother Geta, and in the end Caracalla killed Geta. Some say this ultimate manifestation of sibling rivalry happened when Geta was actually being held in his mother's arms. It seems that the murderous older brother had looks to match his brutal nature – as well as 'Caracalla', he also went by the nick-name 'Tarautas', after a famously ugly and brutal gladiator.

The death of a Roman emperor at York, in the presence of a son who became his successor, was repeated in 306, when Constantius Chlorus died in that city and Constantine was declared emperor.

The church historian Eusebius gives us a detailed account of the persecutions at Alexandria in Egypt under Severus, which happened at the time when the theologian and biblical scholar Origen was growing up there. Origen's father Leonidas was executed under Severus, but not before his enthusiastic son had written him a letter intended to stiffen his resolve to become a martyr. Other Alexandrian victims included the beautiful and chaste Potamiaena, who died after boiling pitch was slowly poured onto various parts of her body.

The Emperor Diocletian, who was responsible for the persecution in which many think Alban died, was in many ways a remarkably good emperor. Edward Gibbon, in the first volume of his *Decline and fall of the Roman Empire*, gives Diocletian a pretty favourable press, praising his good sense and moderation, but not failing to mention his extreme caution and cunning.

It was Diocletian who realised that the Roman Empire was too big, and had too many enemies on its borders, to be ruled by one man alone. He brought in the aforementioned system whereby the empire would be ruled by four men: two Augusti, with two Caesars ruling under them, each Augustus being in charge of half of the empire, which was split into western and eastern halves.

Under Diocletian, the eastern Augustus was the superior one, and this was of course Diocletian himself. His western Augustus was Maximian, mentioned above, who called himself Herculius after the god Hercules. Diocletian took the name Jovius, after Jove or Jupiter, the chief god of the Pagan Romans.

As western emperor, Maximian was based at Milan in Italy, while Diocletian stayed at Nicomedia in what is now Turkey. It was here that a series of events led to Diocletian's persecution of the Christians. The story is told in *The manner in which the persecutors died*, written by a Christian called Lactantius (c.240-c.320).

It seems that, in the traditional way of the Romans before they became Christians, Diocletian employed priests called haruspices to foretell the future from the steaming entrails of recently-sacrificed animals. Readers of Shakespeare will remember that, on the morning of Julius Caesar's assassination, the haruspices can't find 'a heart within the beast'. Likewise, in Seneca's Latin version of *Oedipus*, the misfortunes that are to befall the eponymous hero are predicted by the various details of a sacrifice, including the embryo of a calf discovered growing inside a virgin heifer.

The description of the sacrifice in Seneca's *Oedipus* is prolonged and revolting. Manto, the daughter of the prophet Tiresias, has to pull out the hot entrails of the sacrificial victims and search for abnormalities. As well as the anomalous foetus, she also discovers that the heart of one of the animals is too small. Her father Tiresias is also supposed to have been able to tell the future from the behaviour of birds, though he himself was blind. It may be that the savagery and superstition that surrounded the cults of the Pagan Romans drove some believers to the more decorous ceremonies of the Christians, persecuted though they were.

The priests employed by Diocletian couldn't find anything out of the ordinary in the bowels of their sacrifices, which meant that Diocletian was being denied his customary glimpse into the future. Lactantius tells us that the entrails were all normal because the demons that usually altered them were being blocked by the presence of Christians in the service of Diocletian, who made the 'immortal sign' on their foreheads.

Diocletian's chief haruspex, Tages, sensed that some 'profane persons' were obstructing the rites, and this persuaded the emperor to order that everyone in his palace should sacrifice to the Pagan gods, or be whipped.

36

He went further, and ordered that his soldiers should also sacrifice, or be dismissed from the service.

The emperor was persuaded by his son-in-law, the Caesar Galerius, to follow up these relatively mild actions against the Christians with a full-scale persecution. Galerius was partly motivated by his mother, who resented the fact that Christians would not eat at her table when she served up meat that had been sacrificed to idols. At the festival of the god Terminus, in March, the persecution proper started with the destruction of the church in Nicomedia. The next day, according to Lactantius, an edict was published, depriving the Christians of many rights and privileges, and making them liable to be tortured if they refused to sacrifice to idols.

Some versions of the story of St George, patron saint of England (and of many other countries including Greece, Lithuania and Ethiopia) tell of this saint being tortured and beheaded in the first wave of Diocletian's persecutions as he was, supposedly, a soldier in the imperial army, with the exalted rank of tribune and a job as a palace guard.

Butler tells us that when George heard about the persecutions, he went straight to the emperor and declared himself a Christian. Knowing George to be one of his best officers, Diocletian offered him land, money and slaves, if only he would sacrifice to the Pagan idols. George of course refused, and was taken off to be tortured on a 'wheel of swords' and at last beheaded.

The fourth-century church historian Eusebius of Caesarea wrote at length about the persecutions of Diocletian in his *History of the Church*. Because of when and where he lived, Eusebius had seen some of these horrors with his own eyes.

In many places, the persecutions were wholesale massacres, sometimes carried out in an atmosphere of such hysterical chaos that ghastly mistakes were made. Victims who *had* sacrificed to the idols would be accidentally tortured and killed, while those who declared themselves to be Christians and *refused* to sacrifice were freed by mistake. Ingenious means of torturing, and then killing, Christians were devised: the most horrible method of execution was the technique of tying a victim to two trees that had been bent together, then cutting the trees apart so that the victim would suddenly be torn in two.

Many, like Alban, went calmly and even willingly to their deaths. Given the prolonged mayhem that was happening in parts of the empire, Alban was lucky to have been dispatched so quickly, if it is true that he was killed at this time.

It is interesting that the Christians who were persecuted under Diocletian were in effect tortured and executed because of something they *refused* to do. It is almost as if the Roman authorities didn't mind if they worshipped the Christian God, as long as they were prepared to perform some token sacrifice to the Pagan gods as well. In his *Christianity in Roman Britain to AD 500*, Charles Thomas describes how the Romans feared that the existence of people within their empire who did not sacrifice to the Pagan gods might upset the *pax deorum*, the 'peace treaty' the Romans had made with their gods. Under the *pax deorum*, the gods were understood to be helping the Romans, as long as the Romans themselves kept up the customary sacrifices.

The Pagan gods were also bound up in the Roman imperial state, as Roman emperors were routinely deified after their deaths, and were thought to be able to intercede with the major gods on behalf of Romans who were still alive. One exception to the rule of deification after death was the cult of the emperor Claudius, the successful invader of Britain who was worshipped during his life at a large temple in Colchester.

If it is true that St Alban perished in the persecution of Diocletian early in the fourth century, then the date of his death adds an extra note of tragedy to his story. It may have been only a decade after the martyrdom of St Alban that the Emperor Constantine issued his famous Edict of Milan, removing all the legal disadvantages that the Christians had lived under, and restoring confiscated property to the church. It is not known when, or even if, Constantine was baptised himself, but under his regime it became a positive advantage to be a Christian.

As we know, Bede tells us that when Christianity came to be tolerated, a magnificent church was raised around Alban's remains, a church which was still there in Bede's time. This and other details, such as the story of the visit of St Germanus, have caused modern historians to speculate that the cult of Alban may have continued at St Albans in an unbroken line from Roman times right through to the present day, despite the fact that the town by the river Ver moved east during the intervening centuries. This would seem to contradict the idea that Roman civilisation was completely wiped out when the Romans withdrew from Britain early in the fifth century, and also the theory that the thread of British culture was broken by the spread of the Anglo-Saxons.

# V: NICHOLAS BREAKSPEAR

Very little survives of the Saxon abbey that Offa founded, or of its church. In another wave of invasion, England, which had already been conquered by the Romans and by the Anglo-Saxons, was re-conquered by the Normans in the eleventh century, and it was the Normans who began the church we know as St Albans Cathedral today.

Offa's dream of a religious foundation at St Albans that would rival Canterbury was in part realised when the Catholic world came to be ruled by an English pope. Nicholas Breakspear was born near St Albans, probably in the village of Abbot's Langley, around 1100. The story goes that he was refused entry to the abbey of St Albans on the grounds that he was too young to be a monk, and needed more education. Somehow, Nicholas managed to get to the continent, where he continued his studies and eventually became a canon, then the abbot, of a monastery near Avignon.

Thanks to the patronage of Pope Eugenius III, Nicholas enjoyed a rapid rise in the ranks of the church, becoming Cardinal Bishop of Albano near Rome: the fact that he had gone from St Albans to a place with the similar name of Albano was not lost on Nicholas. As a Cardinal Bishop, Breakspear was sent as papal legate to Scandinavia, where he put the Norwegian church on a better footing, and sorted out a potentially dangerous dispute over the succession to the Norwegian throne. On his triumphal return from the northern fastness in 1154, he was elected pope, taking the name Hadrian (or Adrian) IV.

Shortly after news of the election of the first (and only) English pope reached St Albans, the then abbot, Robert de Gorron, set off to visit Hadrian. They eventually met at Benevento, where Robert presented the new pontiff with a gift of money, gold, silver, and pontifical vestments, including five copes, three mitres and some sandals made by the hermit, Christina of Markyate.

Hadrian responded to these gifts with words the like of which Abbot Robert had no doubt heard repeatedly in his nightmares along the way. The pope said, 'I refuse to take your gifts, for when I fled to your monastery and requested the monastic habit, you refused to receive me'.

The abbot might have responded by saying that he hadn't been abbot at that time, but instead he made the best possible reply that could have been made under the circumstances; 'The reason we were not able to accept you was that the will of God opposed it and His wisdom has directed your life to another path'. Hadrian replied, 'It is not possible for the Blessed Alban to refuse his citizens of St Albans anything'.

Robert de Gorron had not come to Italy laden with gifts expecting nothing in return. He wanted the pope to confer certain privileges on his abbey, to confirm privileges granted by previous popes and, in particular, to remove from his abbey the influence of the Bishop of Lincoln, who assumed a lot of power over the ancient community at St Albans.

Hadrian IV answered the abbot's prayers in full, and his successor as pope continued the pattern of sending papal documents to England, guaranteeing the independence, the supremacy, and the income, of St Albans Abbey. The 'cells' of St Albans, meaning other monasteries ruled from Alban's abbey, enjoyed similar privileges. When a parliament was called, the abbot of St Albans always took precedence over the other 'mitred abbots'. At the time of the Dissolution of the Monasteries under Henry VIII, the annual income of St Albans was valued at £2102, worth nearly £650,000 today.

## VI: GEORGE OR ALBAN?

From time to time, reservations are expressed in England about our country's patron saint, St George. Why was a Roman soldier, who was not born in what became England, made into our patron saint, when we have so many fine home-grown saints?

The reason for the choice of George as patron is obscure – there is a theory that crusader knights, returning from the east, brought the cult with them, along with the white flag with the red cross. The crusader knights, who were once regarded as brave warriors for Christ, are now thought of by some historians as the barbarian invaders of some highly civilized Islamic countries.

St George is also the patron saint of several other countries including, of course, Georgia. He was not patron saint of England until 1348, when he replaced Edward the Confessor, our patron saint for nearly two hundred years.

The fact that George was a soldier and killed a dragon sits uneasily in the minds of some English Christians who consider themselves to be disciples of the Prince of Peace, and value all forms of life.

St Alban would make a good new patron saint for England, not least because he was a man who was not afraid to change his mind, and because the act that led to his martyrdom was an act of hospitality directed at someone who was probably a stranger at first. Of course, if St Alban were to be adopted as patron saint of England, the design of both the English and the Union flags would have to change, and England football fans would have to paint gold saltires, or diagonal crosses, on their faces instead of red upright crosses.

The problem with any choice of Alban as patron saint of England would of course be that, when he was martyred on that flowery hill over seventeen hundred years ago, there was no such place as England, and the English, or Angles, lived elsewhere.

# APPENDIX: BEDE'S VERSION OF
# THE STORY OF ST ALBAN

## From the *Ecclesiastical history*, Book 1, Chapter 7

During this persecution, one of the most illustrious of those who suffered death for the faith, was St. Alban, of whom the Priest Fortunatus, in the book which he wrote in commendation of Virgins, speaking of the great number of martyrs who were sent to heaven by it from every part of the world, says,

> Albanum egregium fæcunda Britannia profert.

> (Fruitful Britain holy Alban yields.)

He was yet a Pagan, when the cruel Emperors first published their edicts against the Christians, and when he received a clergyman flying from his persecutors into his house as an asylum. Having observed that his guest spent whole days and nights in continual praying and watching, he felt himself on a sudden inspired by the grace of God, and began to emulate so glorious an example of faith and piety, and being leisurely instructed by his wholesome admonitions, casting off the darkness of idolatry, he became a Christian in all sincerity of heart.

And, when he had exercised his hospitality towards the before-mentioned clergyman, for some days, a report reached the ears of the impious prince, that the confessor of Christ, to whom the glory of martyrdom had not yet been granted, was concealed in Alban's house: upon which, he commanded some soldiers to make a strict search after him. When they came to his house, St. Alban immediately presented himself to them, dressed in the clothes which his guest and instructor usually wore. Now it happened that the Judge, at the time when Alban was carried before him, was standing at the altar, and offering sacrifice to the Dæmons. And, when he saw Alban, being much enraged at his having presumed, of his own accord, to deliver himself into the hands of the soldiers, and incur the danger of being put to death, he ordered him to be dragged to the idols of Devils, before which he stood, saying, "Because you have chosen to conceal a rebellious and sacrilegious person, rather than to deliver him up to the soldiers, that he might suffer the punishment due to him, for despising and blaspheming the gods—you shall undergo all the punishment, which was to have been inflicted on him, if you refuse to comply with the rites of our religion."

But St. Alban, who had before voluntarily professed himself a Christian to the persecutors of the faith, was not the least intimidated at the prince's threats; but,

44

being armed with the armor of the spiritual warfare, plainly told him that, he would not obey his commands. "Then," said the judge, "of what family or descent are you?" "What does it concern you," answered Alban, "of what family I am? But if you desire to hear the truth of my religion, be it known unto you, that I am now a Christian, and employ my time in the practice of Christian duties." "I ask your name?" said the judge, "which tell me immediately." "I am called Alban by my parents," he replied, "and ever worship and adore the true and living God, who created all things." Then the judge, in a rage, said, "If you will enjoy the happiness of eternal life, do not delay to offer sacrifice to the great gods." To which Alban answered, "Those sacrifices, which you offer to devils, can neither avail the offerers any thing, nor obtain for them the effect of their petitions; on the contrary, whosoever offers sacrifices to these idols, shall receive the eternal pains of hell for his reward." The judge, on hearing him say these words, was exasperated even to fury. He therefore ordered the holy confessor of God to be scourged by the executioners, thinking that stripes would shake that constancy of heart which words could not affect. But he bore the greatest torments for our Lord, not only patiently, but joyfully.

When the judge perceived that he was not to be overcome by tortures, or withdrawn from the profession of the Christian religion, he sentenced him to be beheaded. Being led to execution, he came to a river, which was divided at the place where he was to suffer with a wall and sand, and the stream was very rapid. Here he saw a multitude of persons of both sexes, and of all ages and ranks, who were doubtless assembled by a divine impulse, to attend the most blessed confessor and martyr; and had so occupied the bridge on the river, as to render it almost impossible for him and all of them to pass over it that evening. Almost every body flocking out of the city to see the execution, the judge, who remained in it, was left without any attendance.

St. Alban therefore, whose mind was filled with an ardent desire to arrive quickly at his martyrdom, approached to the stream, and, lifting up his eyes to heaven, addressed his prayer to the Almighty; when, behold, he saw the water immediately recede, and leave the bed of the river dry, for them to pass over. The executioner, who was to have beheaded him among the rest, observing this prodigy, hastened to meet him at the place of execution; and, being moved by divine inspiration, threw down the drawn sword which he carried, and prostrated himself at his feet, earnestly desiring that he might rather suffer death, with or for the martyr, than be constrained to take away the life of so holy a man. Whilst he of a persecutor became a companion in the true faith, and the rest of the executioners hesitated to take up the sword from the ground, the most venerable confessor of God ascended a hill with the throng.

This very pleasant place was about half a mile from the river, enamelled with a great variety of flowers, or rather quite covered with them; where there was no part very steep or craggy, but the whole of it was levelled by nature, like the sea when it is calm: which beautiful and agreeable appearance seemed to render it fit and worthy to be enriched and sanctified with the martyr's blood. When St. Alban had reached the summit of this hill, he prayed to God to give him water; and immediately, an ever-flowing spring rose at his feet, the course being confined; so that every one might perceive that the river had been before obedient to the martyr. For it could not be supposed that he would ask for water at the top of the hill, who had not left it in the river below, unless he had been convinced that it was expedient for the glory of God that he should do so. That river, nevertheless, having been made subservient to the martyr's devotion, and performed the office which he enjoined it, returned; and continued to flow in its natural course as before.

Here, therefore, this most valiant martyr, being beheaded, received the crown of life which God has promised to those who love him. But the executioner, who was so wicked as to embrue his sacrilegious hands in the martyr's sacred blood, was not permitted to rejoice at his death; for his eyes dropped to the ground at the same moment as the blessed martyr's head. At the same time was also beheaded there, the soldier, who before, through a divine inspiration, had refused to execute the sentence on the martyr - concerning whom it is evident, that, though he was not baptized at the baptismal font, yet he was cleansed with the laver of his own blood, and made worthy to enter into the kingdom of heaven.

The judge then, astonished at the novelty of so many heavenly miracles, ordered that the persecution should cease immediately, beginning thus to honour the saints for their patience and constancy, in suffering that death by the terrors of which he had expected to have withdrawn them from their adherence to the Christian faith. St. Alban suffered on the 20th of June, near the city of Verulam, now, from him, called St. Alban's; a church of most exquisite workmanship, and suitable to commemorate his martyrdom, having been afterwards erected there as soon as peace was restored to the Christian church; in which place there cease not to this day the miraculous cures of many sick persons, and the frequent working of wonders.

At the same time suffered Aaron and Julius, inhabitants of the city of Leicester [or Caerleon], and many others of both sexes, in other places; who, having been tormented on the rack till their members were dislocated, and having endured various other unheard-of cruelties, yielded their souls, after the conflict was over, to the joys of the city above.

Trans. William Hurst, 1814.

# SELECT BIBLIOGRAPHY

Bede: *The ecclesiastical history of the English people*, Oxford, 1999

Bolton, Brenda and Duggan, Anne J. (eds.): *Adrian IV the English pope (1154-1159)*, Ashgate, 2003

Deanesly, Margaret: *The pre-conquest church in England*, Black, 1961

Eusebius: *A history of the Church from Christ to Constantine* (trans. G.A. Williamson), Penguin, 1989

Geoffrey of Monmouth: *The history of the kings of Britain* (trans. Thorpe, Lewis), Penguin, 1966

Gildas: *On the ruin of Britain* (trans. G.A. Giles), Dodo Press

Hegge, Robert: *The legend of St Cuthbert*, Simon Webb, 2009

Hoare, F.R.(trans.): *The western fathers*, Sheed and Ward, 1954

Hole, Christina: *English shrines and sanctuaries*, Batsford, 1954

Nennius: *The history of the Britons* (trans. J.A. Giles), Forgotten Books

Niblett, Rosalind: *Verulamium: The Roman city of St Albans*, The History Press, 2010

Paris, Matthew: *The illustrated chronicles of Matthew Paris*, Alan Sutton, 1993

Petts, David: *Christianity in Roman Britain*, Tempus, 2003

Pevsner, Nikolaus: *The buildings of England: Hertfordshire*, Penguin, 1953

Runcie, Robert (ed.): *Cathedral and city: St Albans ancient and modern*, Martyn, 1977

Salway, Peter: *A history of Roman Britain*, Oxford, 1993

Sealey, Paul R.: *The Boudican revolt against Rome*, Shire, 2004

Seneca: *Four tragedies and Octavia* (trans. E.F. Watling), Penguin, 1966

Simeon of Durham: *A history of the church of Durham* (trans. Joseph Stevenson), Llanerch, 1993

Stenton, Frank: *Anglo-Saxon England*, Oxford, 1998

Tacitus: *The annals of imperial Rome* (trans. Michael Grant), Guild, 1990

Thomas, Charles: *Christianity in Roman Britain to AD 500*, Batsford, 1985

Webb, J.F. (trans.): *The age of Bede*, Penguin, 1998

Webb, Simon: *In search of Bede*, The Langley Press, 2010

Webb, Simon: *In search of the northern saints*, Simon Webb, 2009

Webb, Simon: *Nicholas Breakspear: The pope from England*, The Langley Press, 2009

# Also by Simon Webb

ISBN: 978-0956455109

ISBN: 978-0956455123

Published by The Langley Press
langleypress@googlemail.com